CAN YOU FIND MY LOVE?

SEASONS

JAN MARQUART

www.CanYouFindMyLove.com

ISBN: 0967578035
ISBN-13: 9780967578033

Cover and Interior by Publish Pros
www.publishpros.com

Other Books by Jan Marquart

FOR ADULTS

Write to Heal

The Mindful Writer, Still the Mind, Free the Pen

The Basket Weaver, a Novel

Kate's Way, a Novel

Echoes from the Womb, a Book for Daughters

Voices from the Land

The Breath of Dawn, a Journey of Everyday Blessings

How to Write From Your Heart (booklet)

How to Write Your Own Memoir (booklet)

A Manual on How to Deal With a Bully in the Workplace

Cracked Open, a Book of Poems

A Writer's Wisdom

To:

_____

NAME

My appreciation to Rich Carnahan, who worked
tirelessly editing the details and photos for this book with me.

And to Aiden, Cole, Alaina, Wil, Christopher and Emily—
the children who tested the book, gave valuable suggestions,
and were generous with their ideas—I send love and hugs.

Thank you.

CAN YOU FIND MY LOVE?

was inspired by two little angels:
Landon James and Evelyn Kirsten.

Their proud parents are my sweet nephew, David Maravel, and his beautiful wife, Shawn Maravel.

I am proud to call them my family.

You have received this book
because someone loves you.

Look closely—you will find love hidden
in everyday things that you might
normally take for granted.

This is what it looks like.

When you find the love I have placed
for you, I hope that it warms your
heart and lets you know how
very special you are.

Pumpkins grow on the ground in **FALL**.

Pumpkins are used to make
jack o'lanterns for Halloween.

CAN YOU FIND MY LOVE?

In **FALL** it rains a lot.

Puddles form when the ground
can't drink anymore.

CAN YOU FIND MY LOVE?

Green leaves turn red, orange, yellow, and brown in the **FALL**.

Leaves change colors when they don't get enough sunlight to stay green.

FALL is a time when the weather
cools down from summer.

Squirrels start storing acorns
so they can still eat when it snows.

CAN YOU FIND MY LOVE?

In **FALL** bears look for caves to sleep in during the cold days of winter.

The bear's cave is called a den.

CAN YOU FIND MY LOVE?

Can you **DRAW** a few other things you see in **FALL**?

WINTER

Drinking hot chocolate can
keep you warm in **WINTER**.

It warms your hands, your mouth,
and your tummy.

In **WINTER** it snows.

Every snowflake is different,
just like every child.

CAN YOU FIND MY LOVE?

In **WINTER** it can be too cold
to grow certain foods outside.

But you can grow tomatoes inside
in a pot on a sunny windowsill.

Most trees lose their leaves in **WINTER**.

The trees have to get ready
for the new leaves that will grow in spring.

CAN YOU FIND MY LOVE?

In **WINTER** most birds fly south where it's warm.

Birds fly south because they can't find insects and nectar from flowers to eat when it's cold.

CAN YOU FIND MY LOVE?

Can you **DRAW** a few other things you see in **WINTER**?

SPRING

In **SPRING** birds get up early and sing.

Boy birds sing to tell other birds
to stay away from their homes.

CAN YOU FIND MY LOVE?

Birds start building nests in **SPRING**.

Nests are made from grass, leaves, paper, plastic, and sticks and serve as homes for their babies.

CAN YOU FIND MY LOVE?

In **SPRING** trees grow buds
on their branches.

Each bud blooms into a leaf or a flower.

In **SPRING** flowers grow up from the ground and some bloom on the water.

A flower that grows on the water is a waterlily.

CAN YOU FIND MY LOVE?

In **SPRING** caterpillars turn into butterflies.

They wrap themselves inside a cocoon,
grow wings, break free, and fly away.

CAN YOU FIND MY LOVE?

Can you **DRAW** a few other things you see in **SPRING**?

SUMMER

In **SUMMER** kids like to play outdoors.

Playing outside is a fun way to stay healthy.

You can sometimes find frogs
around lakes and ponds in **SUMMER**.

Frogs drink water through their skin.

CAN YOU FIND MY LOVE?

SUMMER is the perfect time to go to the beach and play in the waves.

Waves are formed when strong winds blow the ocean water.

CAN YOU FIND MY LOVE?

In **SUMMER** ants are very busy.

Ants build hills to protect
the tunnels they live in underground.

CAN YOU FIND MY LOVE?

The sun is strongest in **SUMMER**.

A hat that shades your face will protect your eyes from the sun's harmful rays.

Can you **DRAW** a few other things you see in **SUMMER**?

Did you look close enough
to find all the love?

From:

_____

NAME

About the Author

Jan Marquart is a psychotherapist and author. She has published 11 books and has had articles, stories, poems, and essays published in various newspapers, journals, and magazines across the United States, Australia, and Europe. She teaches writing for those over fifty, and has taught a dozen writing workshops for Story Circle Network.

Jan has designed a 6-week writing course titled *Unveil the Wounded Self - Write to Heal* which focuses on healing PTSD and has also designed a 6-week writing course titled *The Provocation of Journal Writing* to encourage everyone to write their personal stories. She is currently on her 99th daily journal.

Jan can be contacted at JanMarquart.com, JanMarquartlcsw.wordpress.com and at her personal email address, jan_marquart@yahoo.com.

Her books can be purchased from all major online book retailers.

www.ingramcontent.com/pod-product-compliance
Lightning Source LLC
Chambersburg PA
CBHW062007090426
42811CB00005B/773